P I L

✠

AYLESFORD

Other titles in the Pilgrim Guide series

CANTERBURY	Peter Brett
DURHAM	Stephen Pedley
ELY	Michael Higgins
HOLY ISLAND	David Adam
IONA	Peter Millar
NORWICH	Stephen Platten
RIEVAULX, FOUNTAINS, BYLAND and JERVAULX	Lucy Beckett
ST ALBANS	Bill Ritson
ST DAVID'S	Brendan O'Malley
SALISBURY	Hugh Dickinson
TEWKESBURY	Michael Tavinor
WINCHESTER	Michael Till
YORK	Leslie Stanbridge & John Toy

PILGRIM · GUIDE

AYLESFORD

Father Wilfrid McGreal O. CARM

Illustrated by
May Farrell

CANTERBURY
PRESS
Norwich

First published in 1998 by The Canterbury Press Norwich
(a publishing imprint of Hymns Ancient & Modern Limited
a registered charity)
St Mary's Works, St Mary's Plain
Norwich, Norfolk NR3 3BH

British Library Cataloguing in Publication Data

A catalogue record for this book is available
from the British Library

ISBN 1-85311-228-3

Typeset by Rowland Phototypesetting Ltd,
Bury St Edmunds, Suffolk IP32 6NU
Printed and bound in Great Britain by
Redwood Books, Trowbridge, Wilts

Contents

A PLAN OF THE FRIARS AYLESFORD TODAY

1. THE MAIN COURTYARD.
2. THE PILGRIMS HALL.
3. THE PRIORS HALL.
4. RECEPTION
5. CLOISTERS
6. CLOISTER CHAPEL.
7. SHRINE
8. CHOIR CHAPEL.
9. THE PIAZZA
10. ST. ANNES CHAPEL
11. THE RELIC CHAPEL
12. ST. JOSEPHS CHAPEL
13. THE GATEHOUSE
14. THE ROSARY WAY
15. THE POND
16. CRAFT CENTRE
17. THE BARN TEAROOM + SHOP
18. CONFERENCE CENTRE

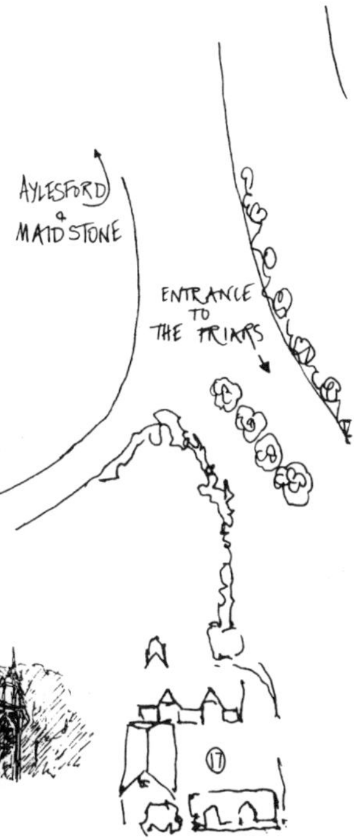

THE BARN TEAROOM + SHOP IN SPRING.

See overleaf also

A plan of the medieval Priory

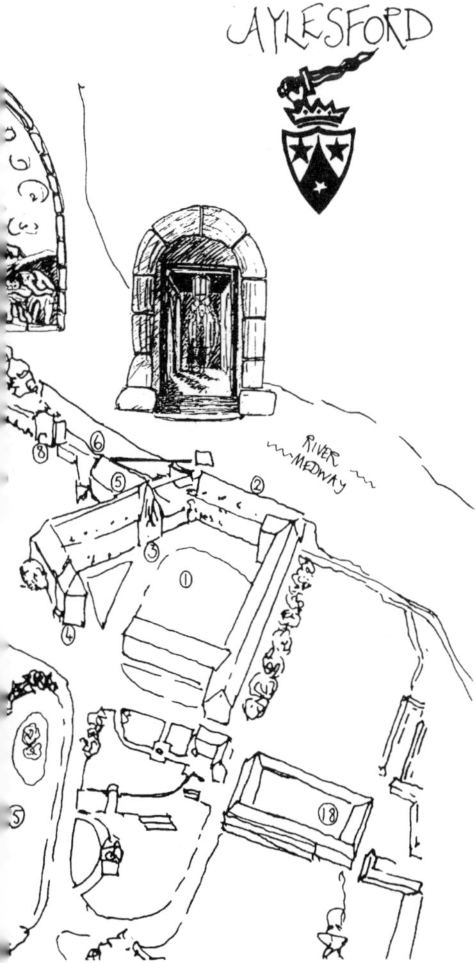
AYLESFORD
RIVER MEDWAY
1
2
3
4
5
6
8
18

Introduction

Anyone travelling along the M20 from London to the coast will see large brown-and-white signs indicating The Friars near the approach to Junction 6. What is The Friars? Who lives there? What is the story of the place? To answer those questions is the purpose of this book. It is a story about people and a place that have played an important part in the life of Kent and continue to do so until this day.

Once travellers leave the rush of the motorway, the signs guide them to the village of Aylesford some three miles north-west of Maidstone. Aylesford, situated on the banks of the River Medway, retains a special charm, with its medieval bridge, its parish church looking down on the village, and a cluster of old houses, some dating back to Tudor times. The Friars is just a few hundred yards north-west of the village at the end of the High Street in a bend of the River Medway.

The Friars is the traditional name for Aylesford Priory, which is home to a Community of Carmelite Friars. The Carmelites first came to Aylesford in 1242, settling on what was then marshy land. They were hermits fleeing persecution in the Holy Land, and they came to England through the good offices of a crusader named Sir Richard de Grey, who gave them a home here in Kent. The newly arrived hermits received a grudging welcome from the local people, especially from the church authorities, who were uneasy about this exotic group. Fortunately, the Bishop of Rochester gave them recognition by allowing them to build a church, which he dedicated in 1248.

At about this time, in 1247, the Carmelites received definitive approval of their Rule by Pope Innocent IV. He confirmed the way of life which the hermits had been following and inserted the Carmelites into the stream of evangelical brotherhoods, making them Mendicant (or begging) Friars like the Franciscans and Dominicans. Today, after 750 years, the Order still flourishes all over the world, but Aylesford has a special place in the Order's story.

The Carmelite Friars spread rapidly throughout Europe. At their height in England they had thirty-nine communities, and their friars were involved in the universities and in preaching up and down the country. Many of the friars became bishops because of their learning. However, when Henry VIII broke with Rome in the 1530s he also put an end to monastic life in England and Wales. The Carmelite Priory at Aylesford was surrendered to the King's Commissioners, and for the next 400 years The Friars was the home of various Kentish families and was caught up in the history of the county.

The Carmelite Friars returned to their old home in 1949. Many of the old monastic buildings were still there, and quickly The Friars became a place of pilgrimage. It was restored by its dynamic and visionary Prior, Father Malachy Lynch, who built the Shrine and put his own creative stamp upon the place.

Today, some fifty years after the return of the Carmelites, The Friars flourishes as a place of pilgrimage and retreat and as an important centre for ecumenical exchange. However, for many, many people The Friars is important as a place where they find peace.

✠

Lord, help me to be open to your peace.
While I am in this place,
may I make a place in my heart for your word.
May your wisdom direct me
so that when I leave this shrine
I can journey in faith and love.

The history of The Friars

From Mount Carmel to Kent

The story of The Friars at Aylesford began in 1242 when Richard de Grey brought a group of Carmelite hermits from Mount Carmel in the Holy Land and gave them a small piece of land at his manor of Aylesford. The Carmelites settled on this marshy land near the River Medway, just north-west of the village of Aylesford and three miles from Maidstone. The newcomers from the Holy Land were not welcomed by the local people, and the first few years must have been difficult.

It seems that the hermits built a small chapel and some individual cells near the river where the present Choir Chapel is situated. It is possible that these first buildings were made of wood. To begin with the Carmelites had no official status – at most they were the guests of the de Grey family. But in 1247 the Bishop of Rochester gave them permission to build a church and to establish a religious house.

1247 was to be a deeply significant year for the Carmelites. In that year the first General Chapter of the Order to be held outside the Holy Land took place at Aylesford. The Chapter elected a Brother

Godfrey as the Prior General but, more importantly, it began a process that would transform the Carmelites from groups of hermits to mendicant friars. This change was not popular with everyone, and it produced tensions between, on the one hand, those who saw a life of prayer and solitude as being more faithful to the Order's vision and, on the other hand, those who saw prayer and service as a seamless whole. It is in this context that St Simon Stock appears.

Very few hard facts are known about St Simon Stock, but he is an important figure in the history of the Order. The story goes that while he was at prayer Mary, the Mother of God, appeared to him in a vision and promised her protection to the new order. She said that the scapular (part of the Carmelite habit) would be the sign of her protection. Simon's vision is said to have taken place at Aylesford in 1251. This episode cannot be proved historically, but it is an important tradition in the Carmelite story and has inspired great devotion to Mary, the Mother of God, both within the Order and in the Church at large.

In 1247 the Carmelites were the beneficiaries of royal generosity. King Henry III gave two marks towards the cost of the chapter that had recently been held at Aylesford. Richard de Grey also helped the Carmelites' finances at this time.

On 31 August 1248 Richard of Wendover, the Bishop of Rochester, dedicated the church at the

Priory in honour of the Blessed Mary, Mother of God, of Mount Carmel and in honour of the Assumption of the Glorious Virgin, thus reflecting the devotion to Mary which the Carmelites had brought with them from the Holy Land. This was one of the first churches in England to be dedicated under the title of the Assumption of Mary. The dedication of this small church, which was quite close to the river, meant that the Carmelites were officially accepted by the local church.

During the next fifty years the Carmelite Order spread throughout the British Isles, with nearly forty priories being established in England alone. By the end of the century the Carmelites – or Whitefriars, as they became known because of their white cloaks – had reached as far north as Aberdeen, and foundations had also been made in Ireland.

✠

We come to you, St Simon Stock,
to ask for your help in our pilgrimage of faith.
Like you, we honour Mary, the Mother of God,
and ask for her patronage.
Obtain for us, through her intercession,
protection and guidance on our journey through life,
so that we may one day reach our home in heaven
and enjoy the blessings of God's peace.

The doorway to the Cloisters

The medieval Carmelites

The Order continued to expand throughout the thirteenth century. However, Aylesford did not become a backwater. It would seem that during most of the medieval period there was a Community of about twenty friars there and, due to local generosity, the Priory became a substantial building. The Pilgrims' Hall was built in about 1280 as a guest-house for pilgrims making their way to Canterbury. Also at about this time a bridge was constructed over the Medway at Aylesford.

Henry de Grey, the first Baron Codnor, proved a generous successor to Richard de Grey, the founder. He left a substantial sum of money to the Carmelites, and this enabled them to improve the accommodation available to the Community.

William Hokiton, the Prior in 1345, initiated plans for the building of a new church. On 13 September 1348 (the Vigil of the Feast of the Holy Cross) the Bishop of Llandaff, John Pascal, who was a Carmelite Friar, blessed the site of the cemetery and the new church. However, the church was not consecrated until 1417. One reason for that would have been the Black Death, which decimated the local population and damaged the economy of the district.

But the Community was not all bricks and mortar. The Prior at this time, Robert St Alban, spent some of the Prior's income on the Library. He bought some manuscripts from John Miller, the parish priest of Aylesford, and also used money from a legacy to build up the Library. In 1381 a list of the books in the Library was drawn up. There were seventy-five volumes, including Bibles, the writings of St Augustine and the *Sentences* of Peter Lombard – all bound in white leather.

One of the more distinguished members of the Order linked to Aylesford Priory is Richard of Maidstone. A doctor of divinity who had studied at Oxford, he was a great controversialist who crossed swords with the Wycliffites. While he was at Oxford he wrote two works attacking the views of John Ashwardby, Vicar of St Mary's, the University Church in Oxford. Ashwardby had criticized the mendicant orders from his pulpit and had urged his congregation to withhold alms from the friars. Richard's argument was that since friars renounced all property so that they could be free to evangelize the world, they had a right to ask for alms. Richard is worthy of note as a religious poet, and his meditative translations of the penitential Psalms were wrongly attributed to Richard Rolle. He died in 1396 and is buried at The Friars.

A provincial chapter or governing body of the Order in England was held at Aylesford in 1407. Thomas Netter, an Essex man, was Provincial and was perhaps the most distinguished friar of his time. He was a confidant of Henry IV and Henry V, but was also a considerable theologian. Netter guided the Province for many years. This was a golden age, a time when the Order flourished and produced some outstanding friars. Shortly after this chapter the Carmelites began to build quite extensively at Aylesford: new cloisters sprang up and many other buildings were radically renovated.

May 1417 saw the dedication of the new church. Richard Young, the Bishop of Rochester, presided at the dedication and also consecrated altars in the church to St John the Baptist, St Peter and St Paul. He also granted forty days' indulgence to all who supported the Carmelites at Aylesford.

The Community continued to receive generous benefactions throughout the century, and this enabled the rebuilding and refurbishing to continue. The dawn of the sixteenth century saw the death of Henry de Grey, the last baron and the end of a line of friends and benefactors. He willed that he should be buried in the chancel of the Priory Church.

In 1505 Peter Terrasse, the Prior General of the Carmelite Order, visited Aylesford. He was a Catalan by birth and had been elected Prior General at a Chapter held in Piacenza in 1503. He made every effort to visit the different houses of the Order, but he was no reformer. He did little to raise standards and granted friars academic degrees without any record of studies being pursued. It seems that Terrasse was more interested in collecting funds than trying to improve the quality of religious observance. By the time of his visit, the English Province of Carmelites had lost much of its vigour.

Local people continued to support The Friars, but by 1534 the clouds were looming. That year all the friars had to make an oath of allegiance to King Henry VIII and Queen Anne, and to swear that the Pope had no more authority than any other bishop. Besides this, their sermons were to be examined for their doctrine and burnt if not Catholic and sound. In addition to the oath, an inventory had to be made of precious objects and movable goods. In 1535, the King's commissioners visited The Friars. The Community held eighteen acres of land worth forty-two shillings and sixpence a year (this seems to have been a low estimate). The end came on 13 December 1538, when Richard Ingworth received the house of Whitefriars at Aylesford into the King's hands. Despite heroic efforts over the years, the Carmelite Friars were not firmly re-established in England until 1926.

Into secular hands

Thomas Cromwell wrote to Sir Thomas Wyatt in February 1539, 'I have reserved for you the house of the Friars of Aylesford.' The Wyatts of Allington Castle, Maidstone, had been loyal supporters of the

Tudors, and Thomas Wyatt was a poet and diplomat of some distinction. He was well rewarded, as he received possession of the Cistercian Abbey at Boxley as well as the Benedictine Convent at West Malling. Some ruins of Boxley Abbey can still be glimpsed from the motorway, but West Malling Abbey once again functions as a religious house.

The Wyatts never lived at Aylesford. In fact, in 1542 the property was leased to John Morse for 40 years at an annual rent of 102 shillings. Thomas Wyatt died in 1542 and was succeeded by his son, Thomas Wyatt the Younger.

The turbulent politics of this period cast a shadow over this part of Kent. Thomas Wyatt opposed the accession of Mary to the throne and joined the Kent Rebellion in 1554. The Rebellion was crushed by forces loyal to the Queen and the ringleaders were executed. The Friars was forfeited to the Crown and was eventually granted in 1570 to John Sedley of Southfleet, who lived at the Priory until his death in 1605.

During his lifetime Sedley began to turn the monastic buildings into a country house. He demolished the Chapel and the section of the Cloister near to the river. He then remodelled the rest of the buildings, putting in new windows. The Refectory Wing over the Cloister Chapel was divided into three floors, and the Gatehouse was built in 1595. The Watergate area was redesigned, providing accommodation for his steward. It is possible that he also built a farmhouse on the site of what is now Lodge Farm. There is a tradition that some of the stone from the Church found its way to Upnor and was used for the strengthening of the fortifications at Upnor Castle. Another tradition has it that Sir Walter Raleigh stayed at The Friars towards the end of the century.

Since John Sedley was childless, when he died his brother, William Sedley, inherited the property. He was made a baronet in 1611. In addition to his charitable works, it seems that Sir William developed the agricultural side of The Friars. A date carved into the door lintel of the recently restored West Barn suggests that it was built in 1615.

Sir William Sedley died in 1619 and his son, Sir John Sedley, inherited the baronetcy and The Friars. However, in 1633 he sold the Priory and 500 acres of land to Sir Peter Rycaut, who came from a Dutch merchant-banking background. The Rycauts were to own The Friars during a turbulent time in English history. The tensions that were to lead to the Civil War were already evident in the 1630s. The Rycauts were firm Royalists, like most of the landowners and people of Kent, but as the county was so near to London, the Parliamentary forces tried to keep a vice-like grip on it. Sir Anthony Weldon, the Parliamentary leader of the county, was able and efficient, but also violent and dictatorial. In 1648 the people of Kent rose up against Parliamentary rule, but in June of that year the rebellion was crushed by Colonel Fairfax at the Battle of Maidstone. For a time The Friars was the centre of Parliamentary control in the county.

Sir Peter Rycaut was exiled from his estate, but was eventually allowed to return. However, afterwards his business collapsed and he became bankrupt. A broken man, he died in 1653 and was buried in St Peter's Church, Aylesford. Lady Rycaut was left with a mountain of debt and was forced to sell The Friars and 512 acres of land to John Banks of Maidstone. The selling price was £8,413.

A wealthy man's mansion

John Banks, the new owner of The Friars, was a Maidstone man. His grandfather was a successful woollen draper who married into a Kentish family of lesser gentry. His father was a leading member of the Maidstone business community, and John Banks inherited the family business acumen. He laid the foundations of his fortune by becoming part of a syndicate set up to victual the Navy. Through his Kent connections he supplied hops, cereal and beef to the Navy, but he also imported canvas and saltpetre from France. At the same time Banks began to underwrite debts, claiming on average some ten per cent for the risk. In this way he could add about £3,000 per year to his income – in modern terms that would be reckoned in millions. His marriage into the Dethick family opened up trading opportunities in Spain and the New World, and he also began to make cautious investments in the East India Company.

The Restoration of Charles II in 1660 could have been a difficult time for Banks, since he had represented Maidstone in the Parliaments of 1654, 1656 and 1659. However, he was pragmatic in his politics and beliefs and so was able to swim with the tide. Like many other businessmen, he saw that a restored monarchy would bring stability, and that was good for business. An example of his pragmatism and his access to hard cash was his willingness to underwrite a debt which Charles II had incurred in Holland. For his service to the new King, Banks was made a Baronet in 1661.

Banks divided his time between London and Aylesford, but it was not until he had established his fortune that he carried out any major alterations at The Friars. In the 1660s he began to purchase land in Burham, Detling and Boxley, and planted some fruit trees. He sold timber and reeds to the Navy and also victualled an expedition to the Mediterranean. With the profits from these sales he was able to build a new barn at Aylesford. Also at about this time Lodge Farm House was built on the site of the old farm building.

During the 1660s Banks began the work of transforming the medieval Priory into an elegant country house. Samuel Pepys was much impressed by the

John Banks's tomb in Aylesford Parish Church

state of The Friars when he called to see Banks on 24 March 1669. Banks was in London, but Pepys reports, 'here I had sight of his seat and house the outside which is an old abbey just like Hitchenbrooke, and as good at least, and mighty finely placed by the river; and he keeps the grounds about it and the walls and house, very handsome. I was mightily pleased with the sight of it.'

Between 1677 and 1679, as a sign that he was one of the 'great in the land', Banks carried out a massive programme of rebuilding The Friars. By 1685 he was able to claim that he had spent the best part of £16,000 on 'land, mansion house and park at Aylesford'.

The lead rain-water heads against the old Refectory and Priors' Hall are dated 1677–8 and so coincide with the building expenditures that Sir John recorded in his account books. The Cloisters were enclosed, new windows were put in and the old stone paving was replaced by black-and-white marble. A new main entrance was made in the east wing, while the old hall was divided into rooms. The west wing on the site of the old Gatehouse was enlarged to include the fine dining-room. The old Refectory became a magnificent ballroom. Here, as elsewhere, beautiful moulded ceilings were put in place, while oak panelling abounded. The decorations of the new ballroom were Dutch in character, so they were unusual in England. Mention is made of Inigo Jones being involved in the decoration of the ballroom. Sir John also lavished care on the gardens, as one can see in the walled garden and the Orangery that remain to this day. A final flourish was the stocking of the deer park.

Sir John lived on until 1699, but his wife and his son Caleb both predeceased him. The Finch family were to be the owners of The Friars for the next two centuries. Heneage Finch was a capable politician who held high office of state. In 1719 King George I made him Earl of Aylesford. The Earl died in that same year, aged seventy, but his wife Elizabeth lived on until 1743. His son Heneage was also involved in political life, and married into a Warwickshire family, the Fishers. His wife Mary inherited the Fisher estates, including Packington Hall. Some time before the middle of the century the Finches made Packington Hall the family seat, and The Friars became the dower house of the family.

The Finch family continued to care for the house and the estate, and sketches made by Thorpe for his study *Antiquities in Kent* (published in 1778) show the Gatehouse and the main Courtyard in excellent order. Thorpe also made a plan of The Friars. His notes make interesting reading; for example, the present-day Pilgrims' Hall is listed as a brewhouse.

The nineteenth century saw a number of tenants living at The Friars, some of whom were retired military officers. For a short period (1847–87) it was again a dower house, as the sixth Countess of Aylesford, Jane Knightly, took up residence. Sir

Arthur Evans, a distinguished paleontologist, stayed at The Friars while he was excavating some Iron Age and Paleolithic sites in the area. Between 1890 and the turn of the century a number of military men rented the property. An advertisement in *The Times* of 19 June 1907 announced that The Friars would be sold by auction on 15 July by Harrods. Clearly the sale never took place, but The Friars suffered a period of neglect in the early years of this century.

A new lease of life

During the First World War a Mrs Woolsey rented The Friars from the Earl of Aylesford's estate. She lived there until her death in 1931. She had a great love of old buildings and began to lavish her time, care and money on The Friars. Her daughter, Alice, and Alice's husband, Copley Hewitt, came to live at The Friars in 1920, and the house came to life again.

Copley Hewitt was an Assistant County Commissioner for the Scouts, and his wife was involved with Guides and Brownies, so it is little wonder that The Friars became an important centre for scouting activities. Lord Baden Powell visited The Friars in 1926.

In his newsletter for September 1965 Father Malachy Lynch records an interesting incident. The Carmelites had returned to Kent in 1926, taking over the Roman Catholic parishes of Faversham and Sittingbourne. The Prior General of the Order, Father Elias Maginnis, visited the county and came over to The Friars in the company of Father Elias Lynch. There was a Girl Guide Jamboree taking place at the time, with the Archbishop of Canterbury as a distinguished guest. Alice Hewitt gave a great welcome to the Prior General.

* * *

A black day in the history of The Friars was 29 June 1930. Fire broke out during the night and a large portion of the house was destroyed. The beautiful moulded ceilings were lost, along with the lovely main staircase. Mrs Woolsey, now an old lady, sat disconsolate near the Gatehouse, watching the house she loved burning. Volunteers carried out valuable paintings and furniture, but many treasures were lost. The south and west wings of the Cloisters were gutted, and a contemporary photograph shows the stone skeleton that remained. Fortunately, the north wing and the Courtyard survived, but the devastation was overwhelming. Mrs Woolsey never recovered from the shock and died some six months later in January 1931.

Mr and Mrs Hewitt, after the initial shock, began the work of restoration. Copley Hewitt negotiated the purchase of The Friars from the estate of the Earl of Aylesford in 1932. The Cloisters were restored to their fifteenth-century splendour, and the old Refectory was given a splendid Gothic window at its west end. Timbers from the old training ship *The Arethusa* were used for the new roof over the Refectory.

While her husband was busy repairing fire damage, Alice Hewitt was able to bring the old chapel in the south wing into use again for worship. In 1935 the Bishop of Rochester gave permission for acts of worship to take place in the chapel. A plaque in what is now the Cloister Chapel records this permission.

Copley Hewitt was not able to complete all the work of restoring The Friars before he died in 1941, aged seventy. During the Second World War servicemen were billeted at The Friars, but the house suffered no damage due to bombing, even though Kent was in the front line during the Battle of Britain.

✠

Lord, when all seems hopeless
and our dreams have turned to ashes,
we ask that our trust shall not falter.
Give us the courage to build anew
and to hope in your providence
that gently shapes our lives
and brings us to a fulfilment
that we could never imagine.

The Carmelites return

After Alice Hewitt's death in 1947, her son, Major Woolsey Hewitt, put the property on the market for sale. Ever since the Carmelites had returned to Kent in 1926, they had hoped that one day The Friars would again belong to the Carmelite Order. Negotiations for the purchase were conducted on 20 June 1949, and the cost was £25,000. The money for the purchase came through an appeal initiated by Father Kilian Lynch, the Prior General of the Order.

The Carmelites returned to The Friars on 31 October 1949. A procession of some fifty Friars wended its way over the old stone bridge through the village and down through the Gatehouse. The

Carmelites feeding ducks

restored Refectory, with its new Gothic window and the great beams from *The Arethusa*, made a fine chapel. After a vigil of prayer, Mass was celebrated on 1 November (All Saints Day), and Father Malachy Lynch was installed as Prior by his brother, Father Kilian Lynch. Father Malachy is a key figure in the story of The Friars. He was an ideal choice as Prior, and for the next decade and more his influence shaped the work of restoration.

The original idea was that The Friars should become a centre of study for the Carmelite Order, but events were to lead the Priory's development down a different road. Father Malachy had only a small Community of Friars and a band of lay helpers that included the newly formed Institute of Our Lady of Mount Carmel. The 'Sisters', as they were called, lived in the Gatehouse, and the friars found space in the main building. Over the next few years the buildings were transformed. A kitchen area was built, and the Pilgrims' Hall was once again a centre for hospitality for visitors. Money and building materials were in short supply, but with Father Malachy's great gift for begging and a sense of trust, the work went ahead.

In 1951 the remains of St Simon Stock were brought back from Bordeaux (where he had died in 1263) to find a final resting place in Kent. The ceremony took place on 16 July with many notable people in attendance. The crowds that flocked to The Friars for the occasion were to become the norm.

The Friars – not by design but by popular choice – was fast becoming a centre for pilgrimage. The first group of pilgrims came from Ealing Abbey in 1950, and soon large groups were coming every Sunday.

The Community of Friars began to grow, and soon workshops and a farm were established. Father Malachy believed that art and beauty were essential for religion. Soon there was a whole group of craftsmen – lay and secular – working at The Friars. Brother Aloysius, a German Carmelite, made tables for the Pilgrims' Hall. Father Brocard Sewell set up a printing press producing elegant books in the tradition of Ditchling. A pottery was established and directed for many years by Brother Michael McMullen. The pots had a simple beauty and wonderful glazes. A farm and market garden began to flourish, thanks to the hard work of two Spanish Carmelites.

Artists were enlisted to add dignity to the restoration work. Philip Lindsay Clarke and his son Michael used their talents as sculptors, and it was Philip Lindsay Clarke who introduced Adam Kossowski to Father Malachy Lynch. Adam had enjoyed a distinguished artistic and academic career in Poland before the War, but during it he had suffered badly, being imprisoned in Central Asia by the Soviets. His first commission was for seven tempera paintings depicting the history of the Carmelites. These hang today in the Chapter Room. Father Malachy then asked him to make fifteen ceramics depicting the Mysteries of the Rosary, to form a garden of prayer for pilgrims. Although Kossowski carried out the commission with some apprehension, it was a success. For some twenty years he continued to work at Aylesford, mainly in ceramics.

In 1951 Father Malachy bought Allington Castle, the former home of Sir Thomas Wyatt. The Castle, two miles upstream from The Friars, became a flourishing retreat centre and remained in Carmelite hands until 1996.

The large numbers of pilgrims gave rise to the question of rebuilding the medieval church. However, Adrian Gilbert Scott designed a large outdoor shrine area with chapels radiating off the central shrine. Work began in 1958 with a few craftsmen and a band of volunteers, plus help from the young friars. Mention must be made of the Italian stonemasons who were crucial to the enterprise. In July 1959 work was well enough advanced for an ordination service to be held in the partly built shrine.

Father Malachy's health began to suffer from the mammoth task, and in 1959 his brother, Father Kilian, who had been Prior General, took over as Prior. He continued the restoration work, helped by Father Malachy, and in July 1965 Cardinal Heenan came to preside at a solemn pontifical Mass of rededication and consecration of the Shrine.

Later that year the River Medway flooded The Friars, causing immense damage to the Courtyard area. Father Richard Hearne, the new Prior, supervised the repair work and began a programme of refurbishing the part of the house occupied by the Community. A fine library was established in the old Refectory area over the Cloister, and conference facilities were established in the new block. The library owes much to the patient work of Father Brocard Sewell, who brought many literary figures to The Friars.

Father Malachy Lynch died in May 1972, worn out by the work of re-establishing The Friars as a Carmelite Priory. At his funeral, Father Edward Maguire, who was to be Prior in the 1980s, asked the question, 'What manner of man was Father Malachy? I would like to think, a combination of medieval mystic and Renaissance prince. He was never daunted.'

In the years since Father Malachy's death, the Carmelite Friars who make up the Community at Aylesford have tried to build on his vision. In the last two decades the work of rebuilding has continued. The great Barn to the west of the main entrance has been turned from a shell into a tea-room and bookshop, and the seventeenth-century farmhouse has been brought back to its former glory. In 1998 some crucial work on the Pilgrims' Hall began. The River Medway has been threatening to undermine it, and as part of an Environment Agency project in conjunction with flood defences, the building is being underpinned.

Most importantly, The Friars has become more and more a part of both the religious life and the social life of the county of Kent. Anglicans, Methodists, Baptists and URC members all come on retreat, and there is also a continuing inter-faith dialogue with Jews and Muslims. Other organizations also enjoy using the facilities at The Friars for meetings and celebrations – the Ambulance Service, the St John Ambulance Brigade, the Fire Brigade and many other groups find a home at The Friars.

During the last 750 years and more The Friars has seen many changes. It has been a place of hope and peace. The history of the county has at times bruised it, but marvellous people like the de Greys, the medieval Carmelites, Sir John Banks, the Copley Hewitts, the twentieth-century Carmelites and the people of Kent have given it life and have never allowed it to die. The spirit of the place – the presence of God and his Saints – has always shone through.

✠

Dear Mother of Carmel,
we pray you to commend to your divine Son
all the cares and anxieties
of those who have asked our prayers:
succour and restore the suffering in body and mind,
pity those who are tried by ill health and disease,
give them light in darkness,

and in your great compassion for the afflicted and unhappy,
lead them close to the strength of Jesus Christ,
your Son our Lord.

Father Malachy Lynch O CARM

Sources

Father Richard Copsey (compiler), *The Friars Aylesford: Chronology of Events 1242–1949* (November 1991, manuscript).

D. C. Coleman, *Sir John Banks: Baronet and Businessman* (Oxford University Press, 1963).

A Rosary Mystery (ceramic)

A tour of the Priory

The superscripted numbers below refer to the plan of The Friars on p. vii-ix.

The entrance to the main Courtyard[1] is the best place to begin a tour of The Friars. The Kentish rag-stone buildings set around the lawn always seem welcoming – especially so in summer, when the late afternoon sun brings out a mellow warmth in the stone. In the medieval period this was the curial court or the back yard of the Priory.

Over the years the buildings to the right, which now serve as accommodation for guests, have seen

The main Courtyard

changes. Sir John Sedley replaced the lower windows and Sir John Banks added dormer windows around 1680. In the far corner of the Courtyard we have the Watergate. Sir John Sedley remodelled this corner to make it a dwelling for his steward.

If you pass under the great arch you will come upon a quay with steps down to the Medway. The Medway was a busy river up to the middle of this century. Produce would have gone by boat from Sir John Banks' estate to victual the Navy at Chatham just a few miles downstream. The river has often burst its banks around Aylesford, and the Environment Agency is busy improving flood defences that will protect The Friars from future damage.

The Pilgrims' Hall[2]

The Pilgrims' Hall which stands next to the Watergate and fronts the river is the oldest building at The Friars. Built about 1280 as a hospice for pilgrims on their way to Canterbury, it is once again a centre for hospitality, acting as a dining-room for guests. Over the years it has been a brewhouse, a forge and a meeting-place for the local scouts and guides.

Up to a hundred people can sit down to meals in the Pilgrims' Hall. The handsome Refectory tables were made in the 1950s by a German Carmelite, Brother Aloysius, and a local craftsman named Charlie Bodiam. On a winter's day logs crackle in the great fireplace, and it is easy to imagine that you have travelled back to the fourteenth century.

The doorways around the Courtyard are all crowned with statues carved by Michael Clarke. St Thomas à Becket and St John Fisher guard the doors leading into the Hall, while Carmelite Saints figure elsewhere in the Courtyard. The Kitchen and the Community Refectory that stand next to the Pilgrims' Hall blend beautifully into the Courtyard. They were, however, built in the early 1950s on the site of an old dairy.

The Pilgrims' Hall

The Prior's Hall[3]

The buildings to our left as we stand at the entrance to the Courtyard house the Reception Office[4] and also what were the Prior's quarters in medieval times. If we walk towards the entrance to the Prior's Hall we come upon a fine fifteenth-century doorway with an old mounting block to the left, and we also see to our left a great archway. This was the entrance to the Courtyard in medieval days and was incorporated into a residential wing built by John Sedley and further developed around 1680 by Sir John Banks. In the upper floor of this wing there is some fine panelling which survived the fire in 1930.

The Prior's Hall would have been the entrance to the medieval Priory, as the rule stated that the Prior should live near the entrance to the Priory so that he could welcome visitors and care for them. Here in the Prior's Hall we have our introduction to the work of Adam Kossowski. Seven tempera paintings depict the history of the Carmelite Order. A door to the right leads to the old Priory kitchen, which is now used as a private dining-room for retreat groups.

The Cloisters[5]

As visitors leave the Prior's Hall they pass into the fifteenth-century Cloisters. Masons' marks can be seen in places. Recent excavations in the Pilgrims' Hall have unearthed masonry with similar marks. Today only half of the Cloisters remain, since during the late sixteenth century the Church and the eastern range were destroyed. Sir John Banks closed in the Cloister arches and made the central arch the main entrance into his house. Lead rain-water heads bearing the date '1678' indicate the period of reordering at The Friars. Part of the Cloister still has its black-and-white marble flooring, but other additions were lost in the fire in 1930. Above the

St Jude – Cloister Chapel

Cloisters is the area where the present-day Carmelites live. Each friar has his own study and bedroom. The medieval Refectory which Sir John Banks turned into a ballroom is now a well-stocked library and a Community sitting-room.

As the visitor walks along the Cloister towards the Shrine, a door leads into the Cloister Chapel.[6] This area was originally set aside for worship by Mrs Alice Hewitt in 1935. Whatever its medieval use may have been, this chapel has a great sense of peace. At the back of it there is a statue of the Infant of Prague which comes from the original convent in that city. In the niche to the right there is a ceramic figure of St Jude by Adam Kossowski. Popular devotion claims that the apostle Jude (also known as Thaddeus) intercedes especially for people who feel desperate. The *Flos Carmeli* window is by the distinguished stained-glass artist Moira Forsyth. She was one of the many artists who gave generous support to Father Malachy Lynch in his work of restoration. The painted Stations of the Cross are by Kossowski.

The Choir Chapel[8]

Visitors now reach the Shrine area designed by Adrian Gilbert Scott, from which a number of chapels radiate. The first chapel the visitor encounters is the Choir Chapel, where the Community gathers for prayer. A great coat of arms hangs over the chapel's entrance. The arms act as a memorial to Archbishop Cyril Cowderoy of Southwark, who was a great friend and supporter of the Community during his time as Archbishop (1950–76). The Carmelites come together for Mass and Divine Office every day, and visitors and guests are welcome to join the Community at prayer. The Choir Chapel is very simple, focused on the altar where Mass is celebrated and the reserved sacrament where pilgrims can pray peacefully.

The Shrine[7]

Beyond the Choir Chapel is the Shrine, dominated by the statue of the Glorious Virgin of the Assumption carved by Michael Clarke in 1960 (he received the Otto Beit medal for sculpture for this work). This powerful yet gentle statue is inspired by the Book of Revelation's reference to the woman with the moon at her feet and the stars around her. Behind the statue some ceramic tiles pick up the vision, and when the statue is floodlit at dusk the combined effect of the statue and the background ceramics is breath-taking. The ceramics and the scaffito work behind the altar are all by Adam Kossowski. One of the angels has been christened 'the Angel of Aylesford', since it holds the Shrine in its arms while its feet are planted in the Medway. The altar frontal is decorated with symbolic ceramics recalling Old Testament worship and the first covenant made by God with Abraham and Moses.

Looking out from the Shrine, we see the Piazza[9] that is filled with pilgrims in the summer-time. White stones in the Piazza outline the site of the medieval Church. Pilgrim groups come to The Friars from all over the South-East, and now that the Channel Tunnel is open, Lille is almost as near as London. Pilgrims come from many different Christian denominations, knowing that they will receive a warm welcome and feel at home. I am sure the medieval Carmelite Friars would have been delighted to know of the vitality and variety of the worship, prayer and welcome that continues in their old home.

The Shrine

✠

Flower of Carmel,
Tall vine, blossom laden,
Splendour of heaven,
Child-bearing, yet maiden,
None equals thee.

Mother so tender,
whom no man didst know,
On Carmel's children
Your favour bestow,
Star of the Sea!

St Anne's Chapel[10]

Just to the right of the main Shrine is a tiny chapel dedicated to St Anne, the mother of Mary. The walls of the chapel are decorated with scraffito work and ceramics that celebrate incidents from the apocryphal Gospel of St James about Joachim and Anne, the grandparents of Jesus. There is a wonderful three-dimensional quality to the work, especially in the ceramic that shows Mary dedicating herself to God's service.

Behind the altar a Renaissance statue attributed to the German artist Reimenschneider shows St Anne holding Jesus and Mary in her arms. The statue came as a gift to The Friars from a Jewish businessman as a thanksgiving for blessings that he had received.

The Relic Chapel[11]

The Relic Chapel is entered through large glass doors. Behind the altar is the reliquary that contains the skull of St Simon Stock. The reliquary, designed by Adam Kossowski, depicts the cells of the hermits on Mount Carmel. Kossowski was very fond of the reliquary because it was for him a special technical achievement, not only of design but also of architectural form. He once suggested that perhaps it should be kept in a less enclosed space.

Some people think the Stations of the Cross in the Relic Chapel are Kossowski's finest work. Certainly, he experienced suffering in his own life, having been imprisoned in a Soviet labour camp after the fall of Poland. The Stations of the Cross are ceramics on a terracotta background. It is worthwhile spending time examining all of the Stations, because each one is alive with amazing detail. Over the altar Kossowski has a 'fifteenth station' – the empty tomb. Here he reminds us that we find the Risen Jesus in our celebration of the Eucharist.

The small chapel to the left is dedicated to the English and Welsh Martyrs. St Thomas à Becket is presented, as are St John Fisher and Thomas More. The walls of the chapel record the names of the forty English and Welsh men and women who died as a result of religious persecution in the sixteenth and seventeenth centuries and were canonized by Pope Paul VI in 1970. A group of Anglican pilgrims contributed to the cost of this chapel as an act of reconciliation.

The Carmelite chapel to the right celebrates Mount Carmel and the Saints of the Carmelite Family. A ceramic on the back wall of the chapel depicts Mount Carmel itself, while underneath the altar there is a representation of the cave of Elijah on Carmel. Above Mount Carmel on the back wall various Carmelite Saints are depicted. St John of the Cross, St Teresa of Avila and St Thérèse of Lisieux figure prominently, while two martyrs from the

Second World War are also remembered – Titus Brandsma and Edith Stein.

The wooden statue in the centre of the chapel is a carving representing the Scapular Vision – Mary appearing to St Simon Stock and promising her protection. Recent research indicates that this statue (probably Flemish in origin) could well be the earliest presentation of this devotion. The statue could well date from the fifteenth century, and so it is fitting that it should have found its way to Aylesford. It was discovered in the 1950s in a Cambridge antique shop and was presented to the Carmelites by Miss Susan Baillie. The statue is a treasured possession and is carried in procession during pilgrimages.

The stained-glass windows in the Relic Chapel are the result of collaboration between Adam Kossowski and Father Norris of Buckfast Abbey. Father Norris uses a method in which thick slabs of glass are welded with concrete and resin, producing bold colours and helpful symbolism. The large hanging lamps were designed by Kossowski and made by a Maidstone smith.

The materials for building the Shrine and the chapels came from various parts of Kent. The tiles for the Relic Chapel roof were no exception. Some came from outhouses at Canterbury Cathedral, others from a Chatham brewery, and yet another batch from the North Pole public house at Offham.

✠

Dear Lord, when looking up to Thee,
I see Thy loving eyes on me;
Love overflows my humble heart,
Knowing what a faithful friend Thou art.

My soul is full of peace and light;
Although in pain this light shines bright.
For here Thou keepest to Thy breast
My longing heart, to find there rest.

For though alone, I have no fear;
Never wert Thou, O Lord, so near.
Sweet Jesus, please, abide with me;
My deepest peace I find in Thee.

Titus Brandsma, Carmelite
(martyred in Dachau, 1942)

St Joseph's Chapel[12]

The final chapel to the left of the Shrine is dedicated to St Joseph, one of the patrons of the Carmelite Order. When restoring Aylesford, Father Malachy would often tell the bank manager, when the overdraft was mounting, that St Joseph would provide. St Joseph's Chapel is often used for ecumenical worship. To the right of the altar is a large statue of the Saint – a strong, vigorous carving, again by Michael Clarke. The ceramics in the chapel are all by Adam Kossowski. Those around the altar show how the universal Church is made up by the communion of local churches. The arch over the altar is decorated with ceramics that tell of Joseph's role in the birth and infancy of Jesus. The ceramics on the wall opposite the entrance depict the transfiguration of Our Lord.

However, the most prominent piece of Kossowski's work in this chapel is the series of ceramics celebrating the great Old Testament prophet Elijah. He is an important figure for Carmelites, since he lived on Mount Carmel, where the Order began. Moreover, his thirst for justice is seen by twentieth-century Carmelites as an inspiration for their lives. The Elijah ceramics have a great sense of energy and dramatic impact.

Scapular Vision – Rosary Way

The Gatehouse[13]

On leaving St Joseph's Chapel visitors come to the Gatehouse. The building as we know it today owes much to the work of Sir John Sedley in the late sixteenth century. At one time a moat which ran round the Priory passed just outside the Gatehouse. Today the Gatehouse is home to a group of dedicated women called Donum Dei, who are part of the Carmelite Family and help in the running of The Friars.

The Rosary Way[14]

If we follow the wall just beyond the Gatehouse we come first of all to a private garden with an orangery. This dates back to the time of Sir John Banks, who not only lavished care on the buildings but also created gardens. Just beyond this garden is the beginning of the Rosary Way, a garden set aside for quiet prayer and reflection. In it a huge London plane tree, which reputedly dates back to the mid-seventeenth century, gives welcome shade in the summer.

Around the garden are ceramics that depict the fifteen mysteries of the Rosary. These small-scale masterpieces were the first ceramics that Adam Kossowski ever produced. Father Malachy Lynch gave him the commission and was so persuasive that the artist did not argue with him, even though the medium was new to him. At the far end of the Rosary Way is a large ceramic shrine celebrating the vision of St Simon Stock. On pilgrimage days the pilgrims process around the Rosary Way, praying the rosary as they do so.

The Gatehouse

✠

Lord give us strength to continue your work
of announcing the Kingdom,
proclaiming justice, working for peace,
living truth and showing mercy in all we do.
We want to work to make the whole of creation
new,
to build a world where all may live in peace and
unity.

Other items of interest

Coming back from the Rosary Way and across the Piazza, visitors come to the Pond.[15] This is all that is left of a series of streams and moats that used to surround The Friars. The Pond is well stocked with fish that occasionally provide a meal for visiting herons! Ducks and swans also inhabit the Pond, to the delight of visitors.

To the south of the Pond there is a range of brick buildings built in the 1950s in traditional Kent style.

The Barn

They include a Conference Centre and accommodation for guests and those who come on retreat. Nearer the river there is a small Craft Centre[16] specializing in pottery and upholstery.

At the entrance to The Friars there is the restored seventeenth-century Barn[17] which, together with the adjacent farmhouse, reminds us of the time when Sir John Banks supplied the Navy at Chatham from his estate at Aylesford. The Barn was until recently in a semi-ruined state and only just survived the gales of 1987. However, it is now beautifully

restored and makes a fine tea-room and shop. The great beams and the thatched roof remind us of traditions of craftsmanship.

To the south and west The Friars is bounded by industry, but to the north there is still the open sweep of the North Downs. To help preserve the tranquillity of the place, the Carmelites are engaged in a major tree-planting project. Already hundreds of trees and bushes have been planted, mostly of traditional deciduous species. The hope is that over the years the environment will be enhanced so that the grounds will provide a sense of peace for all who come. Voluntary organizations are helping us in this, and so too is local industry – especially Aylesford Newsprint, who have been most generous. Also, over the last few years local civil engineering firms have generously helped The Friars by offering their expertise and equipment for projects such as the refurbishment of the Pond.

Window from the Courtyard

The Carmelite Friars today

The superscripted numbers below refer to the plan of The Friars on p. vii-ix.

Friars at the Shrine

Just as it was in the Middle Ages, The Friars today is home to a Community of Carmelite Friars. Twentieth-century Carmelites follow the same Rule as their medieval forebears. While society has seen radical changes, the Carmelites believe that in a place like Aylesford they can bear witness to values that must be constants in our human story.

The medieval Carmelites valued prayer, solitude, study and, above all, the Eucharist, but they also served the surrounding community by sharing their gifts and spiritual insights. We know they were active throughout the north of Kent. Each medieval Carmelite priory had some special work. At Malden in Essex they cared for lepers; at Hitchin they ran a school; and here at Aylesford pilgrims travelling to Canterbury were made welcome.

The Carmelites at Aylesford today welcome pilgrims, preach retreats and listen to people who come with their problems. Young friars often receive some of their initial training at Aylesford. Also, like its medieval counterpart, the present Carmelite Community is engaged in outreach. Friars help with prison ministry, go out to lead retreats and are involved in school activities and chaplaincies. Besides all this, because friars are traditionally preachers, there is also involvement in the media, either through print journalism or local radio and TV. It is this combination of the Community's life of prayer and fraternity, together with a bringing of gospel values to society, that marks out the Friar's life today, just as it did 700 years ago.

The work of caring for pilgrims, those on retreat and conference delegates, means that the Community depends on a team of helpers involved in administration, welcome, catering and maintenance. It is reckoned that over 200,000 people visit The Friars every year. An extended family of helpers enables the Community to make The Friars a place of welcome and to create a sense of community and care – values that are so important in today's society, which can often seem very impersonal.

Today, as in the past, the Carmelite Friars have other communities in Great Britain, ranging from inner-city parishes to university chaplaincies. The Order of Carmelites spreads beyond this country into the four corners of the earth, with communities in countries as far afield as Peru, Indonesia, Zaire and Poland.

The wider Carmelite Family also includes contemplative nuns, sisters involved in a variety of works and lay people who follow the Order's Rule according to their state in life.

Pilgrimages

From April to October every year large groups come on pilgrimage to The Friars to pray at the Shrine, to seek God's blessing and to honour Our Lady. A special pilgrimage leaflet obtainable from the Reception Office gives details of the main pilgrimages throughout the summer, which all are welcome to join.

Anyone wishing to bring a group should contact the Pilgrimage Secretary. Pilgrimages from London are organized on a regular basis. Details can be obtained from Maureen Beck, 50 Alderney Street, London SW1V 4EX.

Retreats

The Carmelite Community runs a programme of retreats; a leaflet giving details is available on request from the Reception Office. Individuals are also welcome to come and join in the prayer life of The Friars. The Community is willing to co-operate in days of recollection for groups who request them and to give help and guidance to schools organizing either days of recollection or residential retreats.

The Guesthouse

The Guesthouse can accommodate up to a hundred people in single or twin rooms. We welcome individuals seeking peace and quiet and groups coming for retreats. For further information please contact the Reception Office.

The Conference Centre[18]

The Friars has a well-established Conference Centre. Its facilities include a main hall seating eighty, three seminar rooms and a bar. We also have several other meeting-rooms for smaller groups. We welcome religious groups, educational courses and business groups. Further details are available from the Conference Centre Administrator.

The Barn Tea-room and Shop[17]

These are located in the restored seventeenth-century Barn. The Tea-room is open all year round and offers a wide range of refreshments and snacks. The Shop sells religious articles and gifts, and the book department has been expanded to make it the most comprehensive Christian bookshop in Kent. Opening times for both the Tea-room and the Shop are: Monday to Saturday, 10 a.m. to 5 p.m. (4 p.m. in winter); Sunday, 11 a.m. to 5 p.m. (4 p.m. in winter).

Address

The Friars, Aylesford, Kent, ME20 7BX.

Telephone and Fax

Tel: 01622 717272. Fax: 01622 715575.